Families

Brothers and Sisters

Revised Edition

Rebecca Rissman

Heinemann Library
Chicago, Illinois

www.capstonepub.com
Visit our website to find out more information about Heinemann-Raintree books.

To order:

☎ Phone 800-747-4992

💻 Visit www.capstonepub.com
to browse our catalog and order online.

Edited by Rebecca Rissman and Catherine Veitch
Designed by Ryan Frieson
Picture research by Tracy Cummins
Originated by Capstone Global Library Ltd

Library of Congress Cataloging-in-Publication Data is available on the Library of Congress website.
ISBN 9781484668306 (pb)

Acknowledgments
We would like to thank the following for permission to reproduce photographs: Getty Images: 10'000 Hours, 5, Edgardo Contreras, 8, Image Source, 19, 23, Karen Moskowitz, 9, Mike Kemp, 13, Mike Tauber, cover, Ron Levine, 10, Ryuichi Sato, 15, Thomas Barwick, 4, Yellow Dog Productions, 17; iStockphoto: Diane Labombarbe, 22, Gary Sludden, 7, James Blinn, back cover, 14, John Prescott, 20, 23, kristian sekulic, 21, Shelly Perry, 6, 23; Shutterstock: Christopher Futcher, 18, Jaren Jai Wicklund, 11, 23, tonobalaguerf, 12, Yuri Arcurs, 16

We would like to thank Anne Pezalla and Nancy Harris for their invaluable help in the preparation of this book.

Every effort has been made to contact copyright holders of any material reproduced in this book. Any omissions will be rectified in subsequent printings if notice is given to the publisher.

Contents

What Is a Family?

A family is a group of people who care for each other.

Families are made up of
different people.

People in families are called
family members.

All families are different.

All families are special.

What Are Families Like?

Families can be big or small.

Families can be loud or quiet.

Brothers and Sisters

sister

brother

There are brothers and sisters in some families.

Brothers and sisters are called siblings.

Girl siblings are called sisters.

Boy siblings are called brothers.

Some brothers and sisters look alike.

Some brothers and sisters
look different.

Some brothers and sisters live with their parents.

Some brothers and sisters live away from their parents.

Some brothers and sisters share the
same parents.

Some brothers and sisters have different parents. They are stepbrothers or stepsisters.

19

Some brothers and sisters are adopted. They have joined a

new family.

Do you have brothers or sisters?

Family Tree

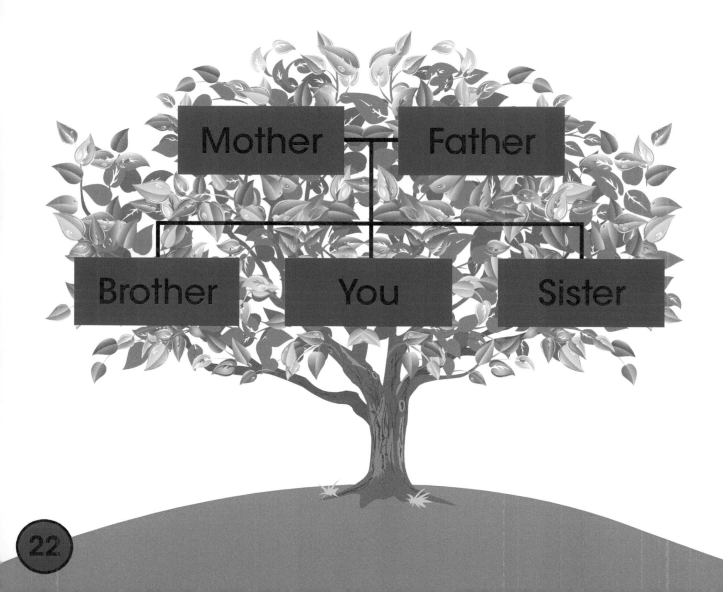

Picture Glossary

 **adopted** invited into a new family. Many families adopt children.

 **member** person who belongs to a group

 **sibling** brother or sister

 **step-brother** or **step-sister** brother or sister with different parents

Index

Note to Parents and Teachers

Before Reading

Explain to children that all families are different. Tell children that some families have only one child, while others have many children. Ask children to name their family members and list any brothers and sisters they might have.

After Reading

• Explain to children that some families adopt children. This means that they welcome a new child into their family. Ask children if they know a family who has adopted a child.

• After reviewing the family tree on page 22, draw a family tree for one volunteer child on the board. Encourage children to go home and draw their own family trees.

24